Praise for

SAGE

"At the height of her poetic powers, Marilyn Chin channels *Sage*, alter ego, orator of sins, praise, urgency, and truth. There is a sharp edge at the end of each epiphany, as fine as a needle, edging close to the heart. Chin approaches national subjects such as democracy, immigration, and injustice as well as the quieter interior subject of artistic creation. *Sage* is a brazen songstress who 'enters the doorless door and breaks the knob,' and by all accounts is as tender as she is powerful, vulnerable as well as mighty. *Sage* reveals our twenty-first-century complexities, straddling ruin and utter magic."
                                                    —Tina Chang, author of *Hybrida*

"A kaleidoscopic, mesmerizing, playful collection of beauty in the vernacular, *Sage* weaves together [Marilyn Chin's] knowledge of ancient traditions and American popular culture. Chin's gifts of Daoist humor, literary scholarship, and, above all, poetic experimentation attest to her attention to form and rebellion. Chin's poetry celebrates, grieves, and even mocks human seriousness about our limited time on earth. She is a poet who witnesses our violences, joys, and human foibles and demands that we do not look away."
                                              —Pamela J. Rader, *Rocky Mountain Review*

T0356619

ALSO BY MARILYN CHIN

POETRY

A Portrait of the Self as Nation

Hard Love Province

Rhapsody in Plain Yellow

Selected Poems (bilingual edition)

The Phoenix Gone, the Terrace Empty

Dwarf Bamboo

FICTION

Revenge of the Mooncake Vixen

TRANSLATION

Ai Qing, *The Selected Poems of Ai Qing* (with Eugene Eoyang)

Gōzō Yoshimasu, *Devil's Wind: A Thousand Steps or More*

CO-EDITED

Dissident Song: A Contemporary Asian American Anthology (with David Wong Louie and Ken Weisner)

Writing from the World (University of Iowa Translation Series)

S A G E

Poems

Marilyn Chin

W. W. NORTON & COMPANY
Independent Publishers Since 1923

"Consultation" artwork reprinted by permission of Heidi Kumao.

For information about permission to reproduce selections from this book,
write to Permissions, W. W. Norton & Company, Inc., 500 Fifth Avenue,
New York, NY 10110

For information about special discounts for bulk purchases, please contact
W. W. Norton Special Sales at specialsales@wwnorton.com or 800-233-4830

Book design by Chris Welch
Manufacturing by Versa Press
Production manager: Lauren Abbate

ISBN 978-1-324-11037-8 pbk.

W. W. Norton & Company, Inc., 500 Fifth Avenue, New York, N.Y. 10110
www.wwnorton.com

W. W. Norton & Company Ltd., 15 Carlisle Street, London W1D 3BS

1 2 3 4 5 6 7 8 9 0

For the Teachers

Some are born to sweet delight
Some are born to endless night

—William Blake

Contents

SAGE

LOOKING FOR THE SAGE

Some say she moved in with her ex-girlfriend in Taiwan
Some say she went to Florida to wrestle alligators

Some say she went to Peach Blossom Spring
To drink tea with Tao Qian

Miho says she's living in Calexico with three cats
And a gerbil named Max

Some say she's just a shadow of the Great Society
A parody
Of what might-have-been

Rhea saw her stark raving mad
Between 23rd and the Avenue of the Americas
Wrapped in a flag!

I swear I saw her floating in a motel pool
Topless, on a plastic manatee, palms up

What in hell was she thinking?

What is poetry? What are stars?
Whence comes the end of suffering?

YOU GO, ME STAY, TWO AUTUMNS
行く我にとゞまる汝に秋二つ

(Masaoka Shiki)

Wipe your lipstick   off the milk carton
Get off your high horse   and wicked palanquin

Dye your ancestral roots   kryptonite DayGlo
Paint your opposable thumbs   Urban decay bonobo

Photo bomb a grief group   confess you're happy
Hang up-side-down off a moonbeam   screech like a banshee

You go   *Me stay*   *two autumns*
You go   *Me stay*   *two autumns*

.

Donne and Keats   scratching tunes   in the kitty litter
Purring poetry and God   thru a negative ion capacitor

Air-hug your Biker neighbor   not too tight   she might bite
Rock roses and jasmine   bathed   in chain-link light

Queen B's a hivin'   Beyond Meat on the barbie
Squid ink gnocchi   6 ft away   still looks nasty

You've been knocking down mojitos
Face-licking boychicks at the Grotto

Auntie's de-coupling   sending you back to Idaho

You go   Me stay   two autumns
You go   Me stay   two autumns

.

Catch a midge in midair   kiss her skinny lips   let go
A raven attacks my wig   He's Edgar Allan Poe

Twittering in twilight   raptors killing doves
Some singing about inequality   some crooning love

Don't fall for the pool boy   ain't got a pool
Don't fall for the girl-boy   can't do ambiguity

But please wear an N95 face mask   if you wanna see me

You go   Me stay   two autumns
You go   Me stay   two autumns

.

June says you're too quiet   Mei Ling   go shout at a rainbow
Adrienne says   Come visit Michelle and me   for Utopian fish gumbo

(Why do I speak to the dead?   'Cause the living are a-holes)

Fat Man   Little Boy   someone will hit bottom
Why worry about Nuclear Winter   our species will be forgotten

You go   Me stay   two autumns
You go   Me stay   two autumns

.

The Princess on the left   says you rhyme with "rich"
The Princess on the right   says your poetry is she-eeet!
Over a million dead   better stay home   you might be next

I'm not funnier than Stevie Smith   waving her undies
Not funnier than Margaret Cho   I'm not that bold
Funnier than Aristophanes?   (The frogs croak no!)

You go   Me stay   two autumns
You go   Me stay   two autumns

.

Is that a 19th-century Mauser   or are you happy to see me?
Don't brag about your viral load   you're a peon amongst peonies

Hating black people   though one is your brother
Hating white people   though one is your mother

Killing racism   like killing lice
Bomb it Raid it   will return   Minnesota Nice

You go   Me stay   two autumns
You go   Me stay   two autumns

.

Visited Granny Wong   in her raised metal bed
Helped her to Root Erase   *Aubergine Drag*

She told this story   (sorry, my translation is bad)

One day whilst shopping at Walmart
A hoodlum grabbed my brocade purse
And called me a stupid old chink!
I chased him down the parking lot
Hooked his ankle with my phoenix-claw cane
Dragged him home in my flying wheelchair
Reciting the dharma of six thieves
Steamed some butterfly shrimp dumplings
In celestial garlic persimmon cream

He gorged three bowls and licked the spoon
Then napped in my La-Z-Boy like a prince
I said, "I'll call your mother to fetch you"
He said, "But my mother is dead"

Praise the mysterious female   mysterious female
Praise the mysterious female   mysterious female

•

I met a masked Vaquera   at the border fair
We line-danced to "Cupid Shuffle"   and "Achy Breaky Heart"

She loved   Selena   Shakira   and Cumbia bands
Don't remember much now   but the pony can dance!

You go   Me stay   two autumns
You go   Me stay   two autumns

I F

(Not by Rudyard Kipling)

If you wear a red dragon on your dress
They'll call you Oriental
If you wear pink jammies in the rain
They'll call you a big baby, and still
Call you Oriental. If you dance naked
Eating plums, plums, plums
With a side of white meat chicken
They'll call you Oriental by way of Williams
If you wear a dragon dress size 18
They'll call you an elephant
If you wear a dead fox on your head
They'll elect you president
Speak in growls and tweets and threats
You are proud to buy American
He'll sell you a piece of Plymouth Rock
And 72 virgins in heaven
Yeah, you are stupid, but you are *our* stupid
If you are pure of blood
You must not be an American
Professor Gates will shake your ancestral tree
And prove that you are half Pangolin
I'd rather be one than eat one
I'd rather eat one than be one

If a conditional marries a conjunctional
You would be a pink-eyed proposition
From the perspective of a gull
We are a raft of tasty excrement

O gray and lonely April day
T.S. Elephant, T.S. Elephant

SAGE

(for Toi, on her 80th Birthday)

Who made the world?

   Vishnu   Raven   Sky Woman   Eiocha   the White Mare
   Pangu   Mawu-Lisa   the cosmic embryo

Who destroyed the world?

Kali
   and her hangry half sisters

Vessel and the realm of non-beings

Who ate the apple?

   Serpent   the all-knowing   eye-teeth
   Audhumla   the synth-cow
   Cornelius   the sun/moon   God-brother

Who saved the world?

   Gaia
   Ella
   Probably Aretha

The babies, the nun-adepts, the spider-mothers

Who saved the world?

Momala   the she-lamb   of Pittsburgh

SAGE

(for Max)

Please don't stop writing poetry
Sad day with no chive dumplings

The lockdown brain is redunkadunk
Gone stale and sump pump ho hum

Ex-lover Proser lost his mojo
Eleventh finger up his bull nose

He sputters baby droplets
Decrying "Yoko, Oh No!"

Attention span of a turd
What did I just say?

I think   I said   a bird

GIRL SAGE

I'm the yellow girl who flunked Algebra
   Calculus, Sudoku, all matter of math

Who shouted "praecepta, excreta!"   on the debate team
   Then, vaped all night   reading Sylvia Plath

Skipped social studies, 'cause, duh, I'm anti-social
   Tik-toked a bloody dance battle   with Norco girl-gang trash

Granny canes me hard
   Makes me kowtow   to some   toothless   clawless ancestor

Brother shouts
   You're a disgrace to our race, loser brat!

Time to escape in my Shaolin jetpack   Avenge the fallen mothership
   Never turn back!

The Sage wears a double-bladed necklace, so what
   The world is unjust

SAGE

(for My Students)

The Sage is a kumquat in yoga pants
She will fight for your honor, or not

She's rocking two layers of a pink hazmat suit
And used stilettos from Saks

The Sage says
Your padre killed my madre's madre
In a reptilian empire ruled by mommadres
Herstory is inexact

The Sage crouches, flashes double swords
    Wipes out poverty, cures racism
    Saves Baby Yoda from Moff Gideon

Sorry, my bad, the Sage cannot!
She enters the doorless door and breaks the knob

ADVICE

(for E)

Be the stealth   between stones
    The abracadabra   among   clones

Be the fighting fish with a fancy tail
    The wizard who   deifies   gnomes

No worry   be happy   missiles flying
    While innocents   are dying

You're pretty nimble   for your age
    One day a wombat   next day   a sage

On the way to feeding a despot
    You summoned   your rage

Most virtuous mother   don't be fooled
    They will bomb our shelter   scorch our earth

Unwind   regroup   turn swine   into pearl
    Be the change   you wanna see   in the girl

DUCK POND ILLUMINATIONS

LOCKDOWN IMPROMPTKU (FOLIO 1)

Boyfriend snoring
On the yoga mat

Who are you fucking
In the underworld?

.

He says you eat batshit
I say I love plums   plums   plums

.

Left hand useless
   Right hand
Strumming
   A flesh guitar

.

No, I am not
Lonely
Denial is a river in Egypt

·

I entered the gateless gate
and stole your vibrator

·

The bell rings
  Buddha
Wagging his tail

·

Hair flowing past my ass
White roots
Tincture of Autumn

·

Revolutions are bloody
Young militants
Sipping Frappuccino

·

A soul tablet flies through air
Decapitates your ancestor

.

Stone by stone
Democracy crumbling
Into a race war

.

Why worry
Just blow your brains
With stinkweed

.

I am not exceptional
I am green

.

Two red ants
Licking up my calf
Not now, little sisters

·

Don't say we are nothing
Year after year
The pear tree blossoms

LOCKDOWN IMPROMPTKU (FOLIO 2)

.

A creepy ghoul moth   a good-for-nothing-cat
    rub against my leggings

.

Half a life   is not an unfinished life   she murmurs

.

Migrant sparrow   on bamboo scaffolding   coughs

.

I sit and sit   until my ass is rotten
    (can't sanitize my mind)

.

She's addicted to *Dae Jang Geum*
    I've succumbed to *Moonlight Resonance*

.

She says   *I love you I hate you*   *You have wasted my life!*
    我愛你, 我恨你, 你浪費了我的生命!

.

At Yonghe Gong   I burned incense at the Great Buddha's toenail

.

Perfume of sick mother   bleach of departed father
    A scent like sea cucumber

.

Death haiku
    Won't you change your strategy

FOLKSONGS
REVISITED

MA' AM, AN AMERICAN TRAGEDY

Ma' am

I know that you are rich
And I'm just a poor immigrant
I've been selling milk tea on the street
Since I was seven
But my grandmother watches me close
From her banana tree in heaven

Ma' am

I dream of a beautiful white house
Can you buy it for me
Give me the keys to the republic?
That baby grand in the window
Some day, I will play it

Ma' am

No matter what you think
I am not after your son
I mean, he's not terribly smart
He's dyslexic and ridiculous
Can't hold a day job
And got a D in calculus

Ma' am

You know your son is odd
He skins cats with his scout knife
He carries around a rubber doll
And calls it his wife

Ma' am

He doesn't love me
Don't worry about it
We just have fun sex
And listen to rap in the basement
I'll go away to a good college
And he'll go to prison

Ma' am

No, he didn't tell on you
Not really, he didn't say
Nothing about your uncle
Or your ex-husband
He didn't tell me much
He just sat there, crying

Ma' am

Did you say "She's war trash
She came from the jungle
She's a weirdo geek, can't
Look up from her books.
Why do you want her?"

Ma' am

Did you say
"Stay away, she's schizoid
Downright ugly
Her father owns that rat-infested roach coach
She'll amount to nothing"

Ma' am

I did not love him, exactly
I did love him too much
It's that in-between-ness
Of love and hate
That made me stuck

Ma' am

I'm gonna love him and drive him crazy
I'm gonna love him though he's lazy
I'm gonna wash his feet and wrap his wounds
Take him off the cross and carry him to his tomb
I'm gonna love him till he hates me
I'm gonna love him and drive him crazy

LOVE STORY

The aerogram says come   the photos show bliss
Another felicitous union   a fresh beginning
He's so handsome fat   she's so new world slim

The envelopes are red   the writing vermeil
He lands a tech job   an iron rice bowl won't break
She's caught a princely man   a silent one   like her father

Sister dyes pink eggs   Auntie boils cider knuckles
The great patriarch is happy   a brand-new grandson
A bundle of joy   from a test tube in heaven

Thank you for your blessings   for your lucky *lai see*
A young girl cares for her now   in a small hospice near the sea
He's alone with the internet   that's where he's happy

WeChat says come   Instagram shows remiss
Thank you for the white gardenias   they'll sweeten his soul
The joss paper boats   will net fish for her   in the next world

THE BALLAD OF STUDENT X

In TJ he downed eight shots of mezcal, ate the worm.
Two prostitutes and a hellhound
Stole his skateboard and hundreds in cash,
Stabbed his friend, while he blacked out in a ditch.

His mother wired me five thousand to bail him out.
He's an animal, a jackass, but he's my student,
If he dies in a TJ prison, he'll be on my conscience.

She said, "He got straight As and decent SATs.
Captain of the football team in junior high.
After my divorce, he went through a bad patch.
Could've been All-American, he's exceptional. Give him a break."

He wrote from rehab, "I found God."
A tweet from a half-way house, he saw Krishna.
At a dude ranch, he shouted Allah on a mountain top.

He cried for salvation, world peace and love.
Some 12-step blather, don't believe a word of it.

Spring break—
He smashed into a tuk-tuk in Chiang Mai,
Maimed an old pedestrian in Phuket.
Plied them with cash,
No questions asked.

"Can you give me an incomplete and comment on my poems?
There's one about my grandmother who died of Covid."
We shared a virtual hug, teared up on Zoom.

Next week, he drove his Beemer off a cliff.
Lucky, he landed on a giant banyan tree,
"Got away without a scratch."

Instagrams of Frat parties, sake bombs at Yuki's,
Arms around bronzed girls in bikinis and sunsets.

"Please, Professor, two more days,
I'm blogging about MLK, writing an opus.
Hand-rolling Maui Wowie
For social justice."

Last week, he came to me in a dream
Dressed for Mortal Kombat, lizard green.
After decapitating a jihadist
And three cleaver-wielding ghouls,

He emerged from a flaming school bus
Showered and shaved.

How we heal this nation, I do not know.
Primal sins erupt through tortured souls.

He graduated with his brothers, magnum cum laude,
Chanting "Liberté, égalité, fraternité! Or death!"

GIRL BOX
SEQUENCE

GIRL BOX

I gaze at the ceiling
I stare at the floor
To my left—sorrow
To my right—a wall

Place three girls in one room
One will laugh
One will cry
One will excel in silence

Some born small
Some born smaller
Some have smallness thrust
Upon them

Deformed, unfinished
Sent before my time
I am subtle, crushed at the edges
I am sublime

Go on, say it
Little Box is not a hoo-ha

Open wide
Hinge back
Scream!
No one is listening

BOX PANTOUM

Can't you dream out of the box?
Marbles rattling in your brain
Your mother was in pain
She said no when she meant yes

Marbles rattling in your brain
You will never amount to anything
She said no when she meant yes
Sickness, death, and despair

You will never amount to anything
Your mother was in pain
Sickness, death, and despair
Can't you dream out of the box?

MERET OPPENHEIM

Little Box does not wear a mink coat
Her name is not Meret Oppenheim

BOX MEASURES

You are a freak, a cuboid
A weirdo trapezoid
A rhomboid ass-wipe
A four-eyed coalition

You are flat as a board
Tit-less as a parallelogram
A straight line   What's your point?
A broken   system

Go back to where you came from

THE GREAT SQUARE

The great square has no corners
The great tone makes a tiny sound
The great image has no form
The Great Mother has no proof

The great square is finally silent
The Long March ends in death
I do not want to die in a box, says mother
I want to laugh in open air

LITTLE GIRL ETUDES

.

They throw stones at the little girls
Over and over they throw stones
They who are their fathers
They who are their brothers

.

They burn the veil of the little girl
The pink one, her favorite
Not too short, not too long
With gilded filigree, they burn it

.

They play Double Dutch with the little girl
Jump, jump
They are surprised by her fast feet
Amazed at her swift tongue

Birdie birdie in the sky
Dropped some whitewash in my eye
Birdie birdie in the sky
Gee, I'm glad that cows don't fly

•

They like to chase the little girl
Up the block, through the narrow alley
Through the barbed wire, onto the roof
Over the train tracks, down the gulch

•

They point their finger at the little girl
They shout, "brat, maggot, whore
Come back and feed your brother
And wash the floor!"

•

They like to hit the little girl
The big one might hit back
And wait till the wee hours
To whack you with an ax

•

They kidnap little girls, Chibok schoolgirls
Make them sex slaves and kitchen slaves
They like to kidnap Yazidi girls
Sabine girls, daughters of Shiloh

•

They like to sell little girls, upriver
For a few pounds of opium, a thousand American dollars
Chained to a bedpost
"Unnamed mother"

·

They like to adopt little girls, from distant orphanages
"They make lovely daughters; the boys aren't easy
They climb the walls and are dyslexic
And the Asian girls are, you know, smarter"

·

They like to bury little girls
Mounds in Nanking, in abandoned churchyards
Around the maquiladoras, along a border fence
Marked by wilted flowers and a crooked cross

·

To everything there is a season
A time to be born, a time to die

A time to kill, a time to heal
A time to grieve, a time to dance

A time to throw stones, a time to gather them
A time for little girls in heaven

FRUIT ETUDES

MELON

Melon is hard on the outside
Tender on the inside
She has a magnificent personality
So, they bred her with an invasive species
Now, she is seedless and childless
Has become uncouth and jokey
She will die on the vine

CHERRY

Her grandmother says Cherry is sweet and kind
If you ruin her, I'll come to your house
Drag you out by your ear
Take a hard branch
Off your crooked ancestry tree and beat you blind

And when I'm dead, I'll haunt you
Curse you
Throw magic spells
Turn you into a hapless
Gonadless monkey
Just for thrills

ONION

(not a fruit)

They chopped off your head during the revolution
Although you have a French passport
I can tell you are a faker from your bad accent
How dare you think that you could float to the top
In the soup of history

PEACH

(for Paul Gaugin)

I shaved off all my fuzz
Even around my navel
Because you are a sick fool
And like shaved girls

You take a first bite
Expecting to get juicy, but instead
You get a mouthful of needles
From a shaman in Tahiti

EGGPLANT

Your mother's eggplant
Kept on the vine too long
Black now, cracked and overripe
Should I throw her out?

Please don't, let's make use of her
For the autumn equinox
We'll dry the belly in the sun
And replant the seeds

BOWL

I'm a cherimoya migrant
Not a crazy rich Asian
Don't put us all into the same bowl
In a tropical Jamba Juice swirl

SUZIE ASADO

Suzie Asado, bitter green tea
Please add honey and make sweet
She was afraid of radiation, upstream
So, she threw out the *Sencha*
Matcha, and *Kombucha*
And kept the *Jasmine Green*
But Suzie, it's laced with arsenic!
The Chinese earth, too, is mean
Now Suzie has recycled her tins
And drinks plain water from a sippy cup

CHAIR, AN INQUIRY

For Christine Blasey Ford

Poem commissioned and inspired by Heidi Kumao's
"Real and Imagined" exhibition
(Stamps Gallery, University of Michigan, 2022)

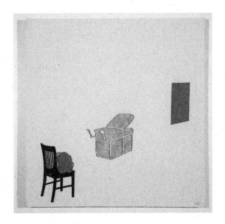

CONSULTATION

Heidi Kumao
"Consultation," 2020
Fabric cutouts, embroidery floss, wool on felt, mounted to wood.
19.25 x 18.75 x 1 in.

CHAIR, AN INQUIRY

For Christine Blasey Ford

1)

A chair   a bed   a girl
A basement   a judge
A chorus   a cry   a long silence

A spotlight   a recollection   a deposition

Riddle:
What has a straight back, four legs, two arms?

Her eternal struggle

2)

Plato: Chair is a perfect form
A copy of a copy of a chair
Is quiet imperfection
A chair has feet and a soul
And acknowledges the mother

Aristotle:
If all red chairs were murdered
The ideal of the red chair
Would disappear from our consciousness

Kierkegaard:
Your truth, my truth
Red chair, black chair

There is only one true chair
The one your ass is sitting on

3)

The chair of the department was a deceitful blob
The chair of the department was lachrymose
The chair of the department was an infidel from Bethesda
The chair of the department has a tiny bullnose
Sorry, we are betwixt and between chairs at the moment
The interim chair is in repose

4)

When Ma Yuan painted bamboo
He became one with the forest

When Kumao paints chairs
She postulates
Suchness

*

Oh
    the sadness
of
    desk chairs
with
    tiny

w.h.e.e.l.s

*

Is Truth, therefore
tyranny
and felt?

Is string theory
Foul matter?

Is an old yarn
A new story?

Your assumptions
Have no legs

We'll assassinate
Your filmographer

Is that a mullet
Or a Schopenhauer?

Is rape
A kind of wildflower?

Truth and lies
One and the same

Good and evil
One and the same

Love and hate
Dao and Chair

5)

Nine chairs facing the camera
Nine chairs of a divided nation

Three branches of government   against the fourth estate
Chairs don't exist   only particles   in perpetual motion

What has a straight back, four legs, two arms?
Swiveling back and forth, cranking up and down

Is a stool a chair?   Certainly not!

The world of forms is perfect!
Copy   of a copy   of your grandma's rocker

Copy   of a copy   of the patriarchy
Copy   of a copy   of black robes
Copy   of a copy   of the fetal   position

Copy   of a transcript   paltry interlocuters
There's no justice in this uncharitable world

What's your reward for speaking out?

You will vanish with a brief cry
He will be sworn in as Overlord

SHADOWLESS
SHADOW

SOLITARY ANIMAL

The solitary animal walks alone. She has no uterus. She has no bone.
She slithers around dark bars and libraries. She carves
a beautiful girl on the cave wall, dances with Aurora Borealis,
but goes home alone.

We are 7.5 billion. Thrust onto earth together, we are not alone.
We shout at the stars, perhaps a Martian is listening, she/he/they
with ten thousand antennae, transversal labia quivering, searching for love.

Your half-drawn monolid eyes are most tantalizing, may I take you home?
Slime you with a green kiss? Breathe magma into your bones? Claw rainbows
onto your lips? Redecorate your home?

Our vertebrae are vibrating, signally: we are not alone. Sacrificed by a greedy
Admiralty, we shall live forlornly, and be devoured, head-first, by reptilian clones.

Inch back into your fern pods, why don't ya! Baby, I call you, but you are not
   home.
Somewhere in the cosmos, our lies are reverberating. Fake news is sad news.
   Shrapnel calcifying

into bone. Each day we begin on earth as a dying person, each breath is
   one less than yesterday, we shall die alone.

SHADOWLESS SHADOW

The Great Matriarch says: There's a dog who barks at his own shadow, which is not there, for in midday sun, there is no shadow.

Notice, if I give him a dumpling or a chew-toy, he stops barking, but he does not stop when he sees his shadowless shadow. He barks with warning, with alarm.

He barks louder and louder, snapping his jaws, swallowing sputum, on his haunches, ready to pounce.

He's afraid of what is not there. Like you, Mei Ling, when you wake up, gasping for breath, thinking you might die, that ICE agents will come with a choke-chain.

Poor dear, he wants to protect us from the unseen, the unexpected, the unknowable. This is very bad luck in the neighborhood, to constant-ly hear the harbinger of doom.

Should we, then, euthanize him, put him out of his misery? To prophesize destruction is to invite bad omens, to stare into the abyss.

Or should we calm him, caress him, give him shelter?

Let's call him by his birth name and take away his power. Let's shout,

"Hashtag, No Collusion, Gunboat, Death Star, Apocalypse, Mara, Diabolus, Beelzebub!"

Let's call him, "The one who understands vacuity."

Let's not fear him, but love him, offer the pink leash, for he is your dog and he is mine.

BAMBOO CEILING

Why, hard-working women all over the world hit one every day! Your best friend Mei Ling, for instance, hits one three times a day. It doesn't hurt, so why complain! Hit a hundred, a thousand times; hit linearly, cubically! Hit the bamboo ceiling exponentially, experientially. You should be glad that there is a bamboo ceiling to hit. That there is a way up the scaffolding at all. Otherwise, you might end up groveling on the dirt floor with the rest of the great unwashed.

After all, a "proverbial bamboo ceiling" doesn't really exist; it's just a pigment of your imagination. Unless, of course, you happen to live in Malaysia or Indonesia, or Pago Pago, somewhere in the South Pacific; from India to China to Madagascar, through most of Latin America and the Himalayas and sub-Saharan Africa . . . And don't forget the serene dreamscapes of Huangshan and the forest Sagano. Wherein bamboo truly exists not just as an idea but as a sprawling green menace, sprouting ten thousand micro-aggressive cuts into the soul.

Now, hitting a "glass ceiling" might be more painful. It might shatter on your way up the corporate chain-of-command elevator at the kleptocracy. And please, never, never dream too big, like becoming president of the free world! The rejection might be too great! The sharp bits might explode into your eyes and blind you!

Glass might
  cut your eyes

Bamboo is merely
  a slight

No worries
  just ceremony

Look up
  your future is bright

MEMORIAL HAIBUN FOR ATTILA JÓZSEF

Ten years ago, I was sentenced to lifelong incarceration for counter-revolutionary activities: espionage, double-crossing, indecent exposure, fornication, buggery, constant hooliganism, pathological mendacity, and malignant halitosis. I responded to my accusers by saying: *My dear Sirs, how could one man possess so many defects?* My various appeals for pardon were rejected by the Ministry of Internal Affairs. All my 539 letters to the Commander of the Right were returned unopened. Then, while I was eating a meager breakfast of gruel and raisins at the Szieszta prison for the criminally insane, three burly fellows in white gowns busted my door and dragged me north.

Then, one fine spring day, I woke up from a long sleep and stepped out of my sister's house. The sun was dancing through the jalousies and the birds were chirping a silly ditty. The bees were trilling, and the spirits were sighing. The sky was so blue it mimicked the hereafter. My sister was baking a pungent apple pie seeped with cinnamon and ginger. I felt so small yet buoyant under the weight of this beautiful disaster.

I took a long walk through the village and met up with my dead love. First, I forgave her for marrying another man during my long incarceration. We knew that the blame was too great for two small people. We wept quietly in each other's arms, then strolled along the Duna, remembering lost years. When we came to our destination, we ate our savory truffles from the candy store and began undressing for our last embrace. First, I folded my tattered cloak and sweater, then my knee-breeches; and my ghost, in turn, laid down her velvet cape and gown, and then and then, her fragrant under-layers . . .

And we laid our naked bodies in front of the military's new bullet train.

I have no father, no mother
No nation, no god
No lover in my cold bed
No one to bury me when I'm dead

They'll catch me, they'll hang me
The silent earth to cover me
Shards of silvery panic grass
To pierce my pure, pure heart

A REMEMBRANCE FOR DAVID WONG LOUIE

Blessed are thy children Jules and Sogna, possessors of the past, heralds of the future.

Blessed thy true love, thy soulmate Jackie, and her eternal beauty, fragrant black hair of compassion, red lips of merciful sacrifice. Blessed our cozy home, our dream palace of light.

Blessed are thy sister and brothers;

Blessed, Father's Long Island laundromat and Mother's Chinatown Confucius Plaza of moribund rectitude.

Blessed are Zsa Zsa and Genius, piebald creatures, bold and hirsute, rabidly democratic and ridiculous!

Blessed be thy art, thy lushness, thy silences, grueling walls that terrorized the mind.

Blessed that we shall finally write the Great American epic to shame Homer and Proust, humiliate Aristophanes, troll Roth and tickle Hemingway. We shall frolic with the fearless Queequeg and conquer the elusive Great White Whale in the afterlife!

Blessed are the UCLA food trucks steaming with greasy street tacos, frowzy tamales and halo halo!

Blessed is J.R. Seafood, waxing and waning between boiled sacred beef and tepid spirit lobster, godless geoduck, salty smelly fish on reluctant pork paddies from the ancients!

Blessed are capons stuffed with frankincense and myrrh and transmi-
grating black bean sauce uber-mensch souls.

Blessed, the Narrow Roads of Venice—fake, redacted canals of quiet
desperation, of curated miniature jungles, manicured curs and mas-
tiffs, Gondola Teslas, tiny houses that shout transient opulence.

Blessed are the unfinished bamboo floors, decomposing kitchens,
malignant architects, carpenter ants who praise the Lord whilst tun-
neling corridors toward purgatory.

Blessed, the tall tales of the university, their hierarchical splendor and
interior squalor.
Blessed, thy students, blossoming with cumulonimbus purple
adjectives.

Blessed, thy friends, black, brown, pink, yellow, whitish, with eternal
tans, furred, balding, fitfully unencumbered, narcissistic, and mad.

Blessed are the hypocrites, liars, sour-faced poets, littering along the
River Niranjana.
Blessed are the solipsistic fat chefs, that means you, Guy Fieri, why are
you so famous!

Blessed the haters; to whom we send a thousand cuts of good for-
    tune, a thousand drums of cheap Beaujolais! Bottoms up, fools and
    ignoramooses!
For David has slayeth Goliath and has finally achieved transcendence.

Blessed are thy past loves, apologies and a gut laugh.
Blessed are the voice boxes that cannot speak, tongues that cannot taste,
    loins that cannot blossom, limbs that cannot embrace!

Blessed be our body ravaged by disambiguated joy!
Blessed that interstitial loneliness, our ultimate surrender.

南無普光佛

NA MO PU GUANG FO

Bless be the Universal Light Buddha

南無普淨佛

NA MO PU JING FO

Bless Be the Universal Purity Buddha

南無多摩羅跋栴檀香佛

NA MO DUO MO LUO BA ZHAN TAN XIANG FO

Bless be the Aromatic Cassia Sandalwood Buddha

南無大悲光佛

NA MO DA BEI GUANG FO

Bless be the Great Compassionate Buddha of Light

FOR THE MAN WHO TRIED TO KILL US

You culled the herd
Took the weakest   among us

The old   the infirm
The gentle grazers

We are not your mother
Who criticized you   unfairly

Not your girlfriend
Who ghosted   last summer

The nation   neglected you
Filled you with hate

We must turn to
Love

GRATITUDE

I AM YOUR TRANSIENT GUEST

(After a Yuan Dynasty scroll:
"The Departure of Lady Wenji from the Nomad Camp")

I am your transient guest
You are my celestial caravan

This palace is made of sand
This rebel camp reeks of mutton

My wedding veil is a trail of gnats
My robe is a shredded colophon

Cross off my days with a black hare brush
Blot out my eyes with obedience

The camels dream on their knees
The trees are naked servants

War drums, bugles advance
Ghosts are shouldering my palanquin

Who dares to utter the tale of Lady Wenji
Whose history cannot be forgotten

"I'll shout your poems," squawk the vultures
"I'll clean your bones," promise the scorpions

Who murdered my family and maids?
Who drowned my songbirds and kittens?

I was kidnapped by a barbarian king
And ransomed for a hundred thousand!

The minister of the left says,
    "Cut your own throat!"
The minister of the right says,
    "No compassion!"

I say, "Kind sirs, please protect my sons;
    "They are not pure, but they are innocent!"
Ghouls and simurghs   barter at dusk
    Scavenger wolves   howl treason

Oh Soul   Come back   I am calling you!
Oh Soul   Come back   reclaim this human!

Do not speak in delusions   for all are a delusion
Do not speak of grief   for all are aggrieved

I finger my butterfly lute
I strum my fated plectrum

Striking the same   fret   fret   fret
Summoning the museum of heaven

GRATITUDE ON CH'IN'S EDGE

Let grief convert to anger, blunt not the heart.

For M.O.

Lotus: white   silent   fist   flower
Unfurling   on Buddha's palm
Truth   shall erupt   any moment now

Mrs. Wong grows silk flowers   they don't wilt or die
Plastic ones are ugly   to a trained girl's eye

.

Most beautiful girl, don't grow old, don't die
Don't rot in the vase while others thrive
They cut you, then wrap you in a plastic shroud
Scatter your yellow ashes to offend the cosmos

They lionize you, malathion you
Your thorns are cherished by Morticia's clippers
Valentine's Day, birthdays, a garland for caskets
Piss a brief scent then sweeten the garbage

.

Oh, wretched one, your breath is sour this morning
I'll brew a cup of joe for you and kiss your forehead
Turn up the Manilow to lighten your sick bed
No need to speak now, the respirator won't save you

．

The bastard slumped in the chair is the ghost of the emperor
He orders your mother around in the abandoned palace
Even in death, Mother, you cannot shut his pie hole
He spits out rice because the kernels are too hard
Flesh too raw   cabbage too bland   no hot food   on cold food day
Let's poison his pablum   rescue the maiden
Crawl into his leather skin   and change destiny

．

Control me, I'm mad, I'm low on meds
They torture my mind with sonnets about ranunculus
Whitman had a beautiful cock   Emily was more god than love
I'm slurping frog noodles   at an ancient frog pond
I'll teach them proper English like a proper Chinaman

．

Twenty years in this institution and I finally see light
My eyes once shuttered   by whiteboard obedience

I cleaned out my desk   they crossed out my eyes
The pupils circling inward   in search of renaissance

.

I am grateful for Gogol's freaking coat
Made of pleather and New Zealand lambskin
Some wise-ass Chinese girl sewed it   in the economic miracle zone
Some jackass stole it from me   while I was teaching "forms"
Dumped into the garbage bin   marked "recyclable"

.

Let me peel off my skin for you   tanned with eternity's blood
Pocked by uncertainty   walking downcast in sun
California is seasonless   but the sun will burn you senseless
A good place to read "The Banality of Evil"

.

Thank you very much   thank you very much
For my green card   for my freedom
For my second   and third dose
Of comeuppance

But Pikachu says
F U very much   F U you very much
Something got lost in translation

·

Rap and sing nephews, dream big, love hard
Sisters, play the lyre and birth rosy children
Become vice president   of merchandizing   own the store!
Ride the gravy train of light
Be realistic with a tinge of margin
Sometimes the bear eats you   sometimes he eats your
Quince

·

Love the Leviathan   pinch him   make him feel grace
Paint a lovely sunset   slap him on the head
Take off your robe and say   the scars have not healed
If that doesn't work   just walk away from THE MAN

·

The five colors of the sunset make me blind
The five sounds of lyre make me deaf
The five tastes make me lose my sense of taste

How long have you been exiled, Li Bai?
Tu Fu, why did they send you to the outpost?

I come naked   I leave naked
But give me back   my soul!

.

Bow down in submission   and you will be preserved
Be bottom   be motionless   a low-lying delta
Let the predators   think you are dead
Let them plow the wetlands   erect their subdivisions
Let them plant their flag   and dream of the West Indies

.

Beg at the door of eternity   you arrogant Airedale
Scoop the senseless kitty litter   without shame
Who is your nemesis, Dr. Moriarty?   A spy in the poetry academy?
The ailing autarky   of sabotage
And pain

.

Wrestle with Laozi   while listening to Bitch's Brew
Blow my head off says Emily   kill me softly covers Lauryn
The space between life and death is a faint aroma of sadness
The border is closing   at Peach Blossom Spring

．

I bow and bow and say thank you very much
I bow and bow and say love your sister
I bow and bow and say thank you very much
I bow and bow and say forgive your father
I bow and bow and say thank you very much
I bow and bow and say let your freak flags fly
I bow and bow to some   motherless   headless god

．

A low-lying valley am I, old dude, a low-lying valley
Let the white troops ride over   waving tiny red flags
Let the red guards follow   waving tiny white flags
I feel so alone   so alone   so alone
Trapped between the R train   and Voldemort

．

I bow and bow to a waning horizon
I bow and bow to ventilator mist
I bow and bow to blue quietude
I bow and bow to twitter piss
I bow and bow to the night blooming cereus

I bow and bow to her fragile green nape
I bow and bow to the flash of the sickle
I bow to the head of Marie Antoinette

·

Girl poet: all lifelong you honored perfection
But the schoolyard   is foul   lunatic   depraved
They will slay you for being "the heathen chinee!"
For being "the perpetual foreigner!"

·

Thank you   Uncle Zhuangzi   for your diaphanous nightgown
Thank you   Auntie Phillis   for your clarion black dress

Butterfly   fluttering her fake eyelashes
West of Ch'in's edge   is our caravan   of lost dreams

CODA: 2022

Ungrateful immigrant   when will you find love?
    Built them a railroad   but that's not enough

Afraid to wait at the bus stop   Afraid to walk alone
    One shouts, "China Virus!"   One shouts, "Whore!"

Six killed in Atlanta   One crushed by train
    Saber in my handbag   Vengeance in my brain

A poem can't change destiny   It's impotent lux
    Debts of blood   must be paid in blood

BIRTHDAY,
BIRTHDAY,
HURRAY, HURRAY!

19TH AMENDMENT RAGTIME PARADE

Birthday, birthday, hurray, hurray
The 19th Amendment was ratified today

Drum rolls, piano rolls, trumpets bray
The 19th Amendment was ratified today

Left hand bounces, right hand strays
Maestro Joplin is leading the parade

Syncopated hashtags, polyrhythmic goose-steps
Ladies march to Pennsylvania Avenue!

Celebrate, ululate, caterwaul, praise
Women's suffrage is all the rage

Sisters! Mothers! Throw off your bustles
Pedal your pushers to the voting booth

Pram it, waltz it, Studebaker roadster it
Drive your horseless carriage into the fray

Prime your cymbals, flute your skirts
One-step, two-step, kick-ball-change

Castlewalk, Turkey Trot, Grizzly Bear waltz
Argentine Tango, flirty and hot

Mommies, grannies, young and old biddies
Temperance ladies sip bathtub gin

Unmuzzle your girl dogs, Iowa your demi-hogs
Battle-axe polymaths, gangster moms

Susan B. Anthony, Elizabeth Cady Stanton
Lucy Burns and Carrie Chapman Catt

Alice Paul, come one, come all!
Sign the declaration at Seneca Falls!

Dada-faced spinsters, war-bond Prufrocks
Lillian Gish, make a silent wish

Debussy Cakewalk, Rachmaninoff rap
Preternatural hair bobs, hamster wheels

Crescendos, diminuendos, maniacal pianos
Syncopation mad, cut a rug with Dad!

Oompa, tuba, majorette girl power
Baton over Spamalot!

Tiny babies, wearing onesies
Raise your bottles, tater-tots!

Accordion nannies, wash-board symphonies
Timpani glissando!
   The Great War is over!

Victory, freedom, justice, reason
Pikachu, sunflowers, pussy hats

Toss up your skull caps, wide brim feathers
Throwing shade on the seraphim

Hide your cell phones, raise your megaphones!
Speak truth to power
     and vote vote vote!

B-SIDE WARNING

Nitwit legislators, gerrymandering fools
Dimwit commissioners, judicial tools
Toxic senators, unholy congressmen
Halitosis ombudsmen, mayoral tricks
Doom calf demagogues, racketeering mules
Whack-a-mole sheriffs, on the take

Fornicator governators, rakehell collaborators
Tweeter impersonators, racist prigs
Postbellum agitators, hooligan aldermen
Profiteering warmongers, Reconstruction dregs

Better run, rascals   better pray
We'll vote you out   on judgment day!

Better run, rascals   better pray
We'll vote you out   on election day!

FROM A POET'S NOTEBOOK: LATE BIRTHDAY, ALL NIGHT BRUSH PAINTING

Auntie Wu sent me a traditional Chinese ink brush painting kit for my birthday. I received it two weeks late. The postage bears a rosy-cheeked image of the great patriarch Sun Yat Sen. Another image is an equally rosy round-faced Chairman Mao facing east. I can see my auntie, eighty-eight years strong, trudging up the monsoon-drenched streets of Wanchai to her favorite antique art store, cursing the wind.

I open the brown paper wrapping to open a second layer of red joss-paper wrapping to open a third layer of Hello Kitty wrapping, and a pink note card tumbles out. On which—I can see my Auntie's grassy hand in a few lines of beautifully penned blessings in Chinese . . . and these rough words in English:

girl   poet   must   learn   brush   painting

II. Hour of the Dog, 19:00

I open the kit and there in front of me gleaming with wondrous possibilities are the four treasures: ink stone, ink stick, brushes (five of varying sizes), and two reams of rice paper.

I remember, thirty years ago, I got a C– in a class called Chinese Calligraphy and Ink Drawing 101.

My teacher, Professor Cheng, said, "Mei Ling, you don't have the disposition for Chinese brush painting, my dear. You don't understand the concept of *wu wei* and contemplation. Your posture is poor, your hand position is wretched, and your strokes are spastic!"

After hearing this, I left the class in tears and never returned.

I take off my day clothes, strip down to my underpants and put on my oversized Chargers night shirt. I sit prostrate and bow to the Goddess of Mercy and vow to finish the task: to learn the strokes, their order, with patience, with redemption.

III. Hour of the Dog, 21:00

First, I use an eyedropper, squeeze five drops of tap water onto the ink stone and start to grind the ink stick. I grind and grind, in a slow clockwise rhythm, and the ink thickens, black, black and gooey, then I squeeze more water and apply more ink stick and more grinding, I grind and grind . . . and let the alchemy of water, ink, and stone work magic and let the solution set.

Meanwhile, I open a new bottle of cheap prosecco left over from my birthday party. I lay out three hundred sheets of rice paper all over my living room, kitchen, and bedroom floor. All white, unblemished faces staring blankly toward heaven, ready to be soiled. Then I choose a big horsehair brush, seep it with water and ink.

My iPhone is happily waiting in its pink docking station with an all-night playlist, beginning with some old-school soul, R&B, the Supremes, the Miracles, the Spinners, and the Temptations—making me rock my hips left and right and I begin painting simple elemental strokes of bamboo branches. I kneel to paint, stand up, kneel, stand up, dance, strut, shake my booty, kneel again . . . I succumb to the invigorating ritual of supplication: kowtow to the ancient art, forehead touching earth, and stand up to greet the sky.

Then, an atomic CD mix I borrowed from my drag queen bff from Lipstick Disco: Madonna/Bee Gees/Donna Summer/Alien Asian/German Techno/ear-blasting rap. Throw in some Earth, Wind and Fire falsetto funk and I'm grooving.

I continue with hundreds of strokes. I hold my brush vertical, perfectly perpendicular to paper. I use my whole arm, not just my wrist. Then, I angle the brush, and pull the ink across paper. Over and over, each stroke is unique and different, yet each stroke, dot to dot, branch to branch . . . speaks for the collective forest.

Bamboo symbolizes strength and resiliency. It can bend in the fierce winds and return upright after battering storms. It must be painted with strong strokes, without hesitation . . .

Branch   to branch   to branch   to branch

IV. Hour of the Pig, 23:00

Perfect for the occasion, I play the Beatles song "Today's Your Birthday!" Full blast, I repeat the song three times. It goes on and on, pounding, and I dance: gyrating pony, mash potato, twisting, shimmying, jerking, boogaloo, break-dance . . . to loosen up, body and soul.

I continue painting: the bamboo branch now transforming itself into an English letter: the primordial "I," the first slow, wet stroke, pushing down the brush, I dot the i, small letter, seemingly quiet and not egomaniacal. I first bow to the modesty, humility, and dignity of my ancestors. Then, I let the onanistic, American riot girrrrrl vision take over! I write with fast stroke wet brush, gleaming and dripping with force.

i i i i i

I dot each i by twisting and lifting the last stroke . . . I do this over and over, one hundred times. I celebrate myself! I sing myself! Girl Poet inserting my presence, my oracular, first-person identity rant, into the muse of night. Fuck you who hate identity poems, U R nobody! I am nobody too! Everybody's somebody to somebody! You ain't nobody till somebody lover you!

V. Hour of the Rat, 00:00

The music is too loud, too bass-driven! Too mind-blowing. So, I take a break, slow down. Softer jazz:

Miles's *Sketches of Spain*; Coltrane's *My Favorite Things*. Very sweet, light. I begin to negotiate control and freedom.

I paint disjointed old branches; make them knobbed and crooked and ancient, flowing from east to west—capturing the surprising and lyrical turns of phrase—

Nodes and hinges/ plum blossoms/ hints of tiny gray shadows/ half of a peach/ with dark kernel/

Dry brushing/ gestures of sprigs/ heaves of spring bracts/ laden with unnamed orbs of berries/

I squeeze out a few tubes of western watercolor: soft reds and blue-greens and yellows, the Confucian colors, bleed together with various tonal shadings of black and gray,

mimicking the fluidity and the riffs/ the abstract riffs/ upon riffs/ of an ancient harp.

Then, a willow branch, with long long yellow gray flowing hair, flowing beyond page, beyond frame, beyond birth and death, mocking eternity . . .

VI. Hour of the Rat, 1:00. Retrieve reality messages.

Beep: a collection agency calls regarding hospital bill #433. Two weeks ago, I fell off my wedgy shoes and sprained my ankle. $4,000 for an X-ray and a long bandage! Hell no, can't pay! Not yet. Beep! X-Boyfriend calling from Orange County, I bet he wants money, too. He says I owe him three hundred for nabbing his Maneki Neko. No

way, cheater loser! Lucky cat! Mine! Bye, bye! Beep! X-student, rap-
name *Plainview da Rod*, the one who appropriated sacred-beaded, Rasta
green hair? Scion of a local kleptocracy, heir to an oil fortune? Bro
of Alpha Caca Pi? The one who slithered drunk to class on a plati-
num skateboard and failed his poetry exam! *The Iliad* is not a haiku!
He wants a recommendation for dental school. No way! Beep! Do I
want to write a brief tribute for our dearly departed Lucille Clifton,
sad, sad, yes, of course! Do I want to write yet another tribute for my
old teacher Ai, yes, sad, sad, of course! A ghazal for Shahid. A son-
net for Adrienne? Let's pen her a whole crown, Petrarchan! Why are
the poets dying? Dear sister Meena, dying, dying. The fine poets are
dying, the fine poets are dying, dying. Beep. Grandma Wong says
she is coming over tomorrow to make dumplings for the New Year.
She says, "Better clean kitchen, foolish girl, everybody's coming for
dumplings!"

VII. Hour of the Ox, 2:00

I uncork a second bottle of prosecco and pull out the last of my
birthday cake, a chocolate eight-layer Black Forest devil from the
freeze. Volody bought it from Goldilocks, a south county bakery of
Filipino decadence. The cake's a lumbering, over-the-top, tooth-
aching hell-mound.

(Are you gonna eat that?) You bet your borderline diabetic cookie monster I am! My triglycerides are leaping into my demented brain. Fat globes sucking on my waistline.

My hands are sticky with ink, but no matter, I take two fistfuls of cake and stuff them into my mouth. My face smeared with chocolate; my veins pumped with sugar! Glucose blasting into my teeming telomeres. Now, I am really grooving:

Dry pink brush against gray wash: *Orchid   orchid   orchid*

VIII. Hour of the Ox, 3:00

I run out of ink. So, I stuff a new black ink stick into my mouth and chomp down: it's chalky and bitter and makes me gag. I gulp down more prosecco and as the ink mixes with the bubbly, it turns into a black paste in my mouth. I look like a vixen ghoul in a black and white horror film, spitting black blood. The black blood leaks from the corners of my mouth, staining my teeth.

But I keep chomping and dancing, I take off my T-shirt . . . And I am dancing naked to *Chaka Khan, Chaka Khan*, and I spit black ink from my mouth onto my breasts and belly and I rub the black ooze all over my skin. My stomach churns and rebels and I spit up black ink all over the floor.

I dip my brush into my black sputum to create my first Chinese word

heart

Auntie, can you see my aorta? And the valves and the ventricles? Auntie, can you see how my heart is pumping, spitting black blood, just for you?

IX. Hour of the Tiger, 4:00

I fall asleep, flat on my back, on the cold hardwood, legs-up-the-wall corpse pose but am jarred awake by hard metal guitar feedback! Jimi! Jimi! Jimi!

Jimi Hendrix put me in a darker mood: War, Vietnam, death-copters, grenades, body-bags, napalmed forests, soul-anguish!

Jimi playing "Star Spangled Banner" on an empty Woodstock stage with ferocious irony

and might! So, I oblige and leap to my senses—paint Zen and revolution!

Zeros zeros zeros   turn into   *skulls skulls skulls*

How did this happen? Why did darkness explode so violently? How was history changed in one stroke?

Professor Cheng says: *The strokes are irrevocable. Once the ink is laid, there is no revising it. This is not western oil painting, Mei Ling, there's no gessoing over your errors.*

Auntie says, *"Good thoughts. Good intentions. Good actions. Mei Ling, it is never too late to change the world."*

X. Hour of the Tiger, 5:00, Poetess Interruptus. Sex-texting with Volody.

V: Baby, I want to fk, I want to fk now! I wanna tear off my pink cummerbund, leap off the piano! Get naked!

Me: But Volody, you are in Canada!

V: Canada is only a state of mind. My polecat is in a state of mighty erection.

Me: Go take a cold showa, will ya!

Me: Please calm down. Come home and play *Fur Elise* for me soon! *Fur Elise, Fur Elise*. I love that hackneyed piece of goo candy! I love the sweet repetitions.

May we finally contemplate the universe? In a hackneyed gooey way? May we stop pretending to be ironic and hipster cool? I was never cool. Thick coke-bottle glasses and crooked teeth. We were too poor. We had too many crowded teeth or too many missing. The dress was too big or too small. Shoes held by duct tape. We never smiled or smiled in forced compliance with the outer world.

We were too poor for sublinguals. I was OK with the missionary position: you preaching to me from above. I was quite the willing convert.

XI. Coda

On this occasion of the fiftieth anniversary of my birth, two weeks late, I must reverse darkness back into light:

Skull skull skull turn into *frond frond frond* turn into *peach peach peach*

I have finished painting three hundred pages and I consider them to be worthy. I shall let them dry and send the best revelations to my dear old Professor Cheng, who has now resettled in Taiwan, in the township of the Marble Gorges.

Finally, I must punctuate this all-night Chinese ink painting extravaganza with a commemorative haiku:

Turning skulls into peaches

This late American birthday

With love

Acknowledgments

I thank the following commissions and publications for supporting my work.

Commissions

"A Remembrance for David Wong Louie" was recited at his memorial conference at UCLA and was published in the Poetry Society of America website.

"Memorial Haibun for Attila Jószef" was written for the Terezín Music Foundation's celebration honoring the seventieth anniversary of the liberation of Nazi concentration camps.

"19th Amendment Ragtime Parade" was commissioned by the New York Philharmonic and the Academy of American Poets.

"I Am Your Transient Guest" was commissioned by the Smith College Museum of Art to celebrate a Yuan Dynasty scroll called "The Departure of Lady Wenji from the Nomad Camp."

"Chair, an Inquiry" was commissioned by Heidi Kumao and the Stamps Gallery to celebrate Kumao's "Real and Imagined" exhibition.

Publications

Poetry magazine: "Fruit Etudes," "Girl Box," "Little Girl Etudes"
Poem-a-Day: "Sage"
The Paris Review: "Solitary Animal"
Kenyon Review: "You Go, Me Stay, Two Autumns"
Washington Square Review: "From a Poet's Notebook: Late Birthday, All
    Night Brush Painting"
Poets.org: selections from "Lockdown Impromptku"
Los Angeles Review of Books: "Ma' am, an American Tragedy"
Veritas Review: "The Ballad of Student X," "Eggplant," "Suzie Asado"
En Bloc: "Shadowless Shadow"
Civitella Ranieri Anthology: "Bamboo Ceiling"

Gratitude (sincerely, unabashedly)

I thank Robert Grunst, my patient and generous first reader, for
    ingesting my poems whilst traipsing around the Alps. I thank Floyd
    Cheung for taking care of us Asian American poets! Please save us
    from obscurity! I am grateful to the multi-talented David Kater for
    helping me create images in "From a Poet's Notebook: Late Birth-
    day, All Night Brush Painting." I thank the beautiful and brilliant
    Lauri Scheyer for her meticulous reading and for holding my hand
    through the last hours of the manuscript. I thank the hard-working
    families at both the Sandra Dijkstra Literary Agency and at W. W.

Norton. Finally, I thank my dear comrade-sisters Jill Bialosky and Sandy Dijkstra, who have been my supporting angels throughout the years. As the mantra goes: "Sisterhood is powerful!"

I am extremely grateful to the following sponsors who have offered sustenance and aided the completion of this book.

The Ruth Lilly Poetry Prize
The DePauw University Field Professorship
The Mackey Chair at Beloit University
The Louis D. Rubin Chair at Hollins University
The Anisfield-Wolf Book Award
The Corporation of Yaddo
The American Academy of Arts and Letters
The Radcliffe Institute for Advanced Study